DISCOVER!

AMERICA'S AMAZING LANDMARKS

MOUNT RUSHMORE

By Marie Roesser

Enslow PUBLISHING

Please visit our website, www.enslow.com. For a free color catalog of all our high-quality books, call toll free 1-800-398-2504 or fax 1-877-980-4454.

Library of Congress Cataloging-in-Publication Data
Names: Roesser, Marie, author. | O'Mara, Mary, 1939- Visit Mount Rushmore.
Title: Mount Rushmore / Marie Roesser.
Description: New York : Enslow Publishing, 2026. | Series: America's amazing landmarks | Includes bibliographical references and index.
Identifiers: LCCN 2024056728 (print) | LCCN 2024056729 (ebook) | ISBN 9781978543980 (library binding) | ISBN 9781978543973 (paperback) | ISBN 9781978543997 (ebook)
Subjects: LCSH: Mount Rushmore National Memorial (S.D.)–Juvenile literature.
Classification: LCC F657.R8 R647 2026 (print) | LCC F657.R8 (ebook) | DDC 917.8393–dc23/eng/20250203
LC record available at https://lccn.loc.gov/2024056728
LC ebook record available at https://lccn.loc.gov/2024056729

Published in 2026 by
Enslow Publishing
2544 Clinton Street
Buffalo, NY 14224

Portions of this work were originally authored by Mary O'Mara and published as *Visit Mount Rushmore*. All new material this edition authored by Marie Roesser.

Cover Designer: **Nicholas Switalski**
Interior Designer: Rachel Rising
Editor: Therese Shea

Photo credits: Cover, p. 1 Mendenhall Olga/Shutterstock.com; back cover, pp. 1, 3-24 Jeffery Edwards/Shutterstock.com; back cover, pp. 1, 5, 13, 21 Oleksandr Poliashenko/Shutterstock.com; p. 4 Panas Wiwatpanachat/Shutterstock.com; p. 5 Bardocz Peter/Shutterstock.com; p. 6 melissamn/Shutterstock.com; p. 7 Jeffrey M. Frank/Shutterstock.com; p. 9 https://commons.wikimedia.org/wiki/File:Gutzon_Borglum_1919.jpg; p. 11 (Lincoln) https://en.m.wikipedia.org/wiki/File:Abraham_Lincoln_O-77_matte_collodion_print.jpg; p. 11 (Washington) https://en.wikipedia.org/wiki/File:Gilbert_Stuart_Williamstown_Portrait_of_George_Washington.jpg; p. 11 (Jefferson) https://en.wikipedia.org/wiki/File:Official_Presidential_portrait_of_Thomas_Jefferson_(by_Rembrandt_Peale,_1800).jpg; p. 11 (Roosevelt) https://en.wikipedia.org/wiki/File:T_Roosevelt.jpg; pp. 13, 15 National Park Service; p. 14 Fer Gregory/Shutterstock.com; p. 16 Tricky_Shark/Shutterstock.com; p.17 https://en.wikipedia.org/wiki/File:Mount_Rushmore2.jpg; p. 19 https://commons.wikimedia.org/wiki/File:RushmoreWithLeftJefferson.jpg; p. 21 SL-Photography/Shutterstock.com.

Printed in the United States of America

Some of the images in this book illustrate individuals who are models. The depictions do not imply actual situations or events.

CPSIA compliance information: Batch #CSENS26: For further information contact Enslow Publishing, at 1-800-398-2504.

CONTENTS

BOLDFACE WORDS APPEAR IN THE GLOSSARY.

LOOK UP!

Would you want your face on the side of a mountain for all to see? Mount Rushmore National **Memorial** in South Dakota shows the **carved** faces of four U.S. presidents: George Washington, Thomas Jefferson, Theodore Roosevelt, and Abraham Lincoln.

MILLIONS TRAVEL TO SEE MOUNT RUSHMORE EACH YEAR!

ROBINSON'S IDEA

Doane Robinson, the state **historian** of South Dakota, came up with the idea of a giant carving in 1923. He believed a large piece of art in the Black Hills would bring more visitors to his state.

Black Hills

THE SCULPTOR

In 1924, Robinson wrote to **sculptor** Gutzon Borglum. Borglum visited South Dakota. He saw Mount Rushmore, a peak that rose above the surrounding Black Hills. This was the location he chose for a huge monument to U.S. presidents.

Gutzon Borglum

PICKING THE PRESIDENTS

The presidents shown on Mount Rushmore were chosen carefully. Washington **represented** the nation's founding. Jefferson represented its growth. Lincoln was honored for guiding the nation through the **American Civil War**. Roosevelt had helped the United States become a world power.

George Washington

Thomas Jefferson

Abraham Lincoln

Theodore Roosevelt

HARD, DANGEROUS WORK

Work began on Mount Rushmore in October 1927. Each day, workers climbed more than 500 steps to the top of the mountain. A small cable car carried supplies and tools. Workers sometimes hung from cables as they shaped the mountain!

EVEN THOUGH THE WORK WAS DANGEROUS, NO ONE DIED DURING THE CARVING OF THE MEMORIAL.

Gutzon Borglum made a model head of each president. Workers used these **models** to create the presidents' faces on the mountain. First, they used **dynamite** to remove larger pieces of rock. They drilled holes and filled them with the dynamite.

blasting for the Abraham Lincoln carving

Workers also used heavy **jackhammers** to remove stone from the mountain. This prepared the surface for the carvers. The carvers used drills and hammers to make the smaller parts of each president's face. After a day's work, carvers and other workers were covered in **granite** dust.

jackhammer

work on
the George
Washington
carving

OVERCOMING PROBLEMS

There were problems along the way. For example, the first carving of Thomas Jefferson was too heavy. It had to be blasted off the mountain. In March 1941, Gutzon Borglum died. Still, a few months later, the carvings were finally completed.

first carving of Thomas Jefferson

VISIT THE MEMORIAL

Today, visitors to Mount Rushmore can walk toward the memorial on the Avenue of the Flags. They can learn more about the memorial's history in the Hall of Records. The Presidential Trail takes them close to the 60-foot (18.3 m) carvings. Mount Rushmore is a must-see monument!

TODAY'S MEMORIAL HAS MANY SITES FOR PEOPLE TO VISIT AND LEARN ABOUT THE MONUMENT AND U.S. HISTORY.

GLOSSARY

American Civil War: A war fought from 1861 to 1865 within the United States.

carved: Formed by cutting and shaping a material such as stone.

dynamite: A powerful explosive.

granite: A kind of rough, hard rock often used for building.

historian: One whose job is to be knowledgeable about history.

jackhammer: A handheld power tool used for splitting or drilling rock.

memorial: A place, display, or event that serves as a way to remember someone.

model: Something used as an example to follow.

represent: To stand for.

sculptor: An artist who creates shapes with stone, wood, metal, or other matter.

FOR MORE INFORMATION

Books

Culliford, Amy. *Mount Rushmore*. Coral Spring, FL: Seahorse Publishing, 2022.

Goldsworthy, Kaite, and Heather Kissock. *Mount Rushmore*. New York, NY: AV2, 2022.

Websites

Mount Rushmore
www.nps.gov/moru/index.htm
This is the official site of the Mount Rushmore National Memorial.

Mount Rushmore Facts
www.sciencekids.co.nz/sciencefacts/engineering/mountrushmore.html
Read many more fun facts about this American landmark.

Publisher's note to educators and parents: Our editors have carefully reviewed these websites to ensure that they are suitable for students. Many websites change frequently, however, and we cannot guarantee that a site's future contents will continue to meet our high standards of quality and educational value. Be advised that students should be closely supervised whenever they access the internet.

INDEX